For Fred,

new
kids
by lynn goldsmith

You'll always Be
a 'New KiD'
to ME ♡ Lynn

First published in the United States of America
by the PROFESSIONAL PHOTOGRAPHY DIVISION of
EASTMAN KODAK COMPANY and
distributed by RIZZOLI INTERNATIONAL PUBLICATIONS, INC.,
300 Park Avenue South, New York, N.Y. 10010

Fourth Printing

ISBN (hardcover edition): 0-8478-1304-5
ISBN (softcover edition): 0-8478-1305-3

Designed by Elizabeth Van Itallie

Printed and bound in Japan by Dai Nippon Printing Co., Ltd.

pure love

sacred love

unconditional love

this
book is
dedicated
to love

puppy love

true love

real love

universal love

self love

unrequited love

motherly love

brotherly love

endless love

labor of love

new kids o

n the block

by lynn goldsmith

The Professional Photography Division
of Eastman Kodak Company

RIZZOLI
NEW YORK

I first met New Kids On The Block in the spring of 1988. CBS Records sent me their album Hangin' Tough and asked if I would go to Boston to photograph them. After listening, I agreed. They had a sound of innocence which I wanted to capture visually. I will never forget that day because as I did the individual shots, I found myself under the spell of their charisma. Then in the winter of 1990, their manager Dick Scott told me how he'd like to have a strong photographic book on the Kids. Kodak had offered me the opportunity to do a book on whatever I wanted, so a light bulb went on in my head. I thought about how this group had grown since the day that I had met them and how millions of teenage girls now felt the way I did. I'm sure guys like them too, but their concert audiences are filled for the most part with girls who believe that they have found true love. I missed having that kind of love. I wanted to be part of it, see it, get it on film...share it.

What the New Kids had come to represent was another attraction to doing a book. They stood for a Nineties consciousness: an anti-drug stance, the breaking down of racial boundaries, and most importantly, a loving "family" spirit. So I packed my bags and for three months, throughout Canada, the United States, and Europe, I photographed them. I tried to go wherever they went. This was not an easy task since they wanted to have some private time. I showed them the images as we went along and they came to understand what I was trying to do. They let me in. As I became a part of their lives, my feelings for the New Kids grew. I respected how hard they worked, I admired their ability to show their feelings to each other, I was in awe of how many autographs they could give in a day! At the beginning, I would wake up in the morning and wonder who I would fall in love with that day. I was lifted out of my world and placed into another where I could have feelings for them as a girlfriend, a sister, a mother, a friend.

This is not to say that it was always fun. In fact, it was like a rollercoaster ride. When you get on you're excited and a little scared. Then off you go, your heart is pounding with the thrill, but suddenly you're going down faster than you imagined and you wonder why you ever got on the ride in the first place. Just as quickly, it's back up again and you're part of a screaming group and wouldn't want to be anywhere on earth other than where you are. Then without warning, it's straight down and you think to yourself that you must have been crazy to do this, but by the time the car pulls back into the station you're sad it's over – you wish you could all ride together forever and ever.   – Lynn

j

jordan

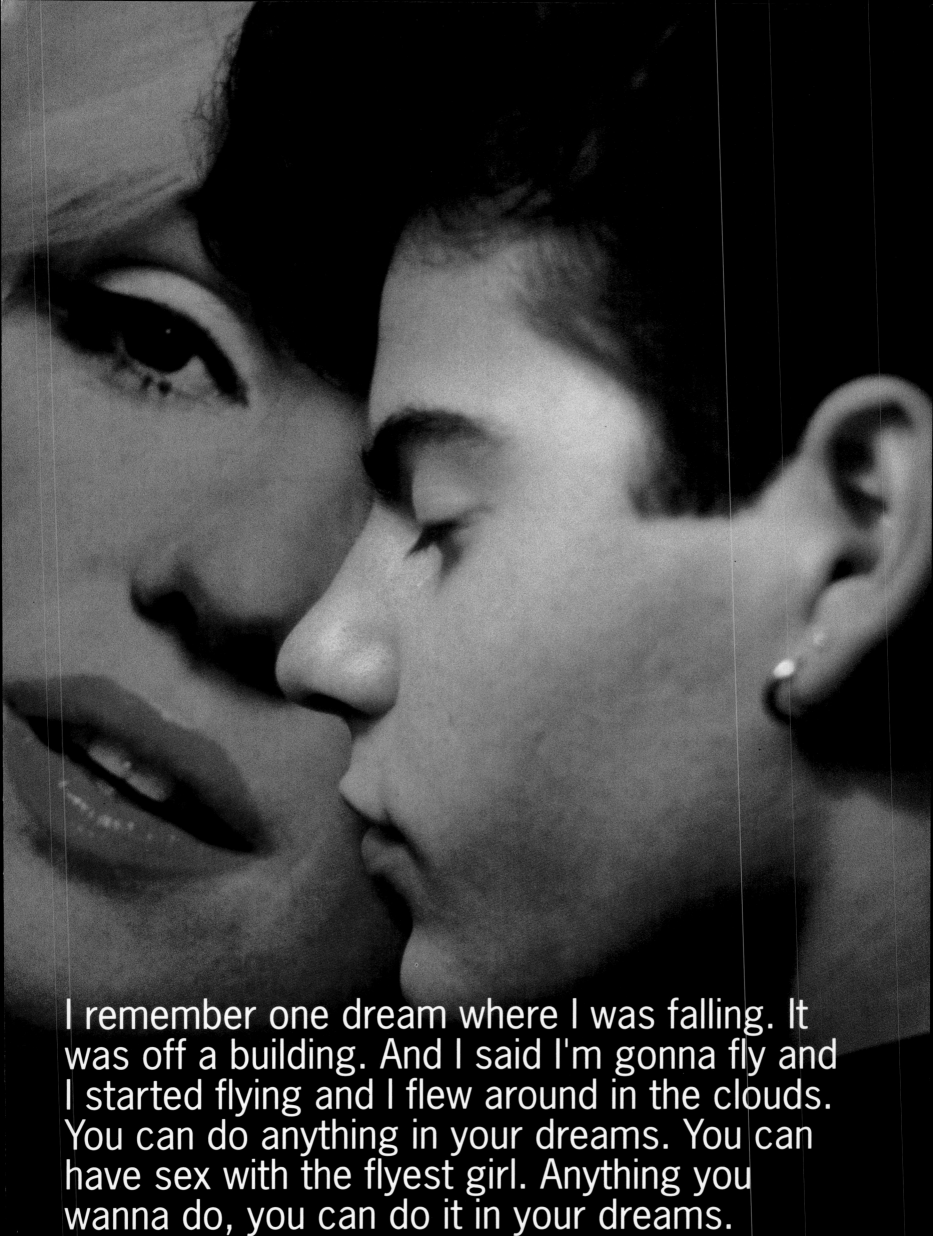

I remember one dream where I was falling. It was off a building. And I said I'm gonna fly and I started flying and I flew around in the clouds. You can do anything in your dreams. You can have sex with the flyest girl. Anything you wanna do, you can do it in your dreams.

I can't give my total self away. I just think I am private.

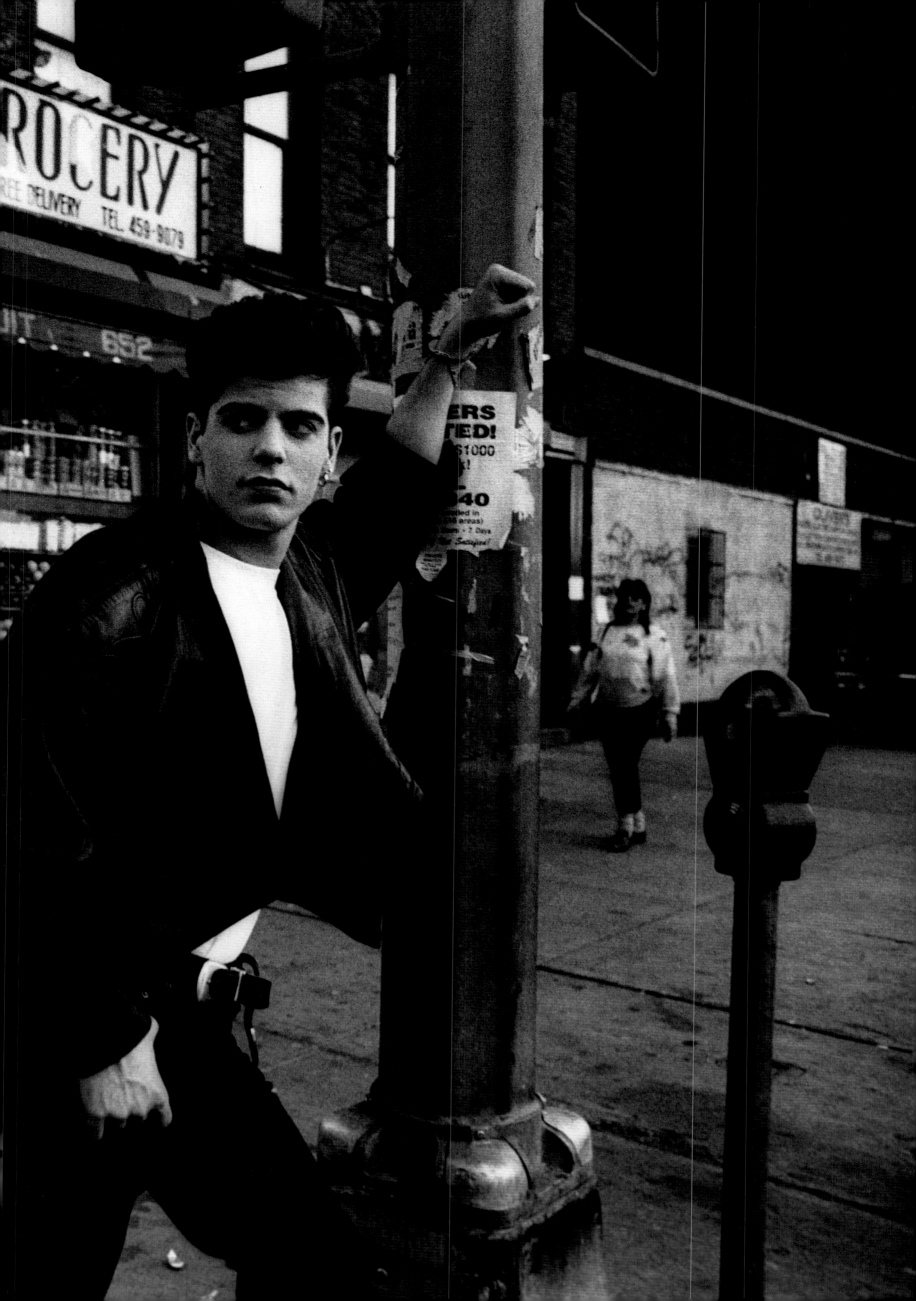

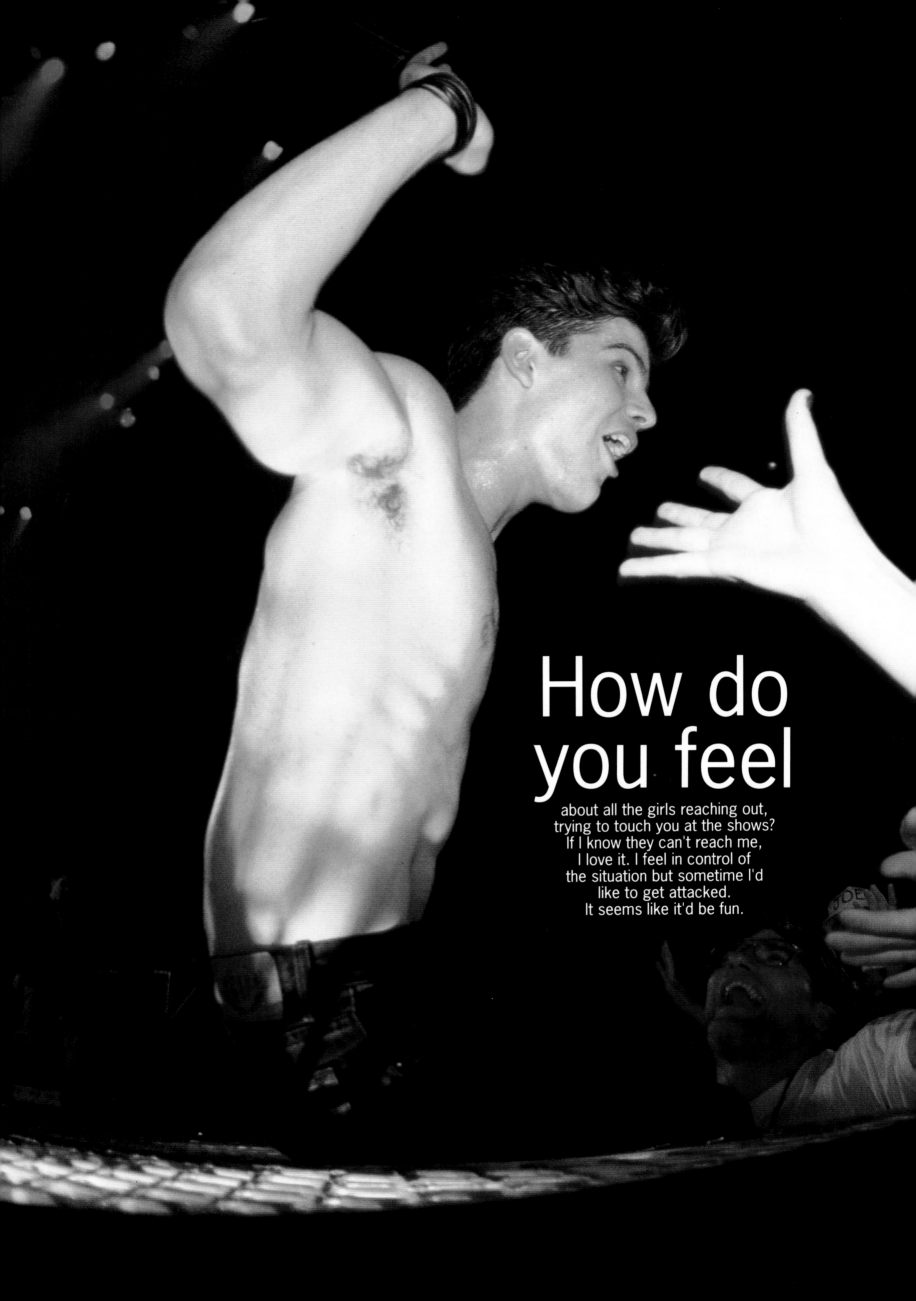

How do you feel

about all the girls reaching out,
trying to touch you at the shows?
If I know they can't reach me,
I love it. I feel in control of
the situation but sometime I'd
like to get attacked.
It seems like it'd be fun.

The worst thing about being
and being all cramped up
something I gotta go through

on the road is being lonely–
in a hotel room. If I want to do
all the security checks.

I'm vulnerable when I'm in love.

Since I was little I always had the feeling something great was going to hap-pen to me. I never really worried about what I was going to do in the future. I felt that God was watching over me.

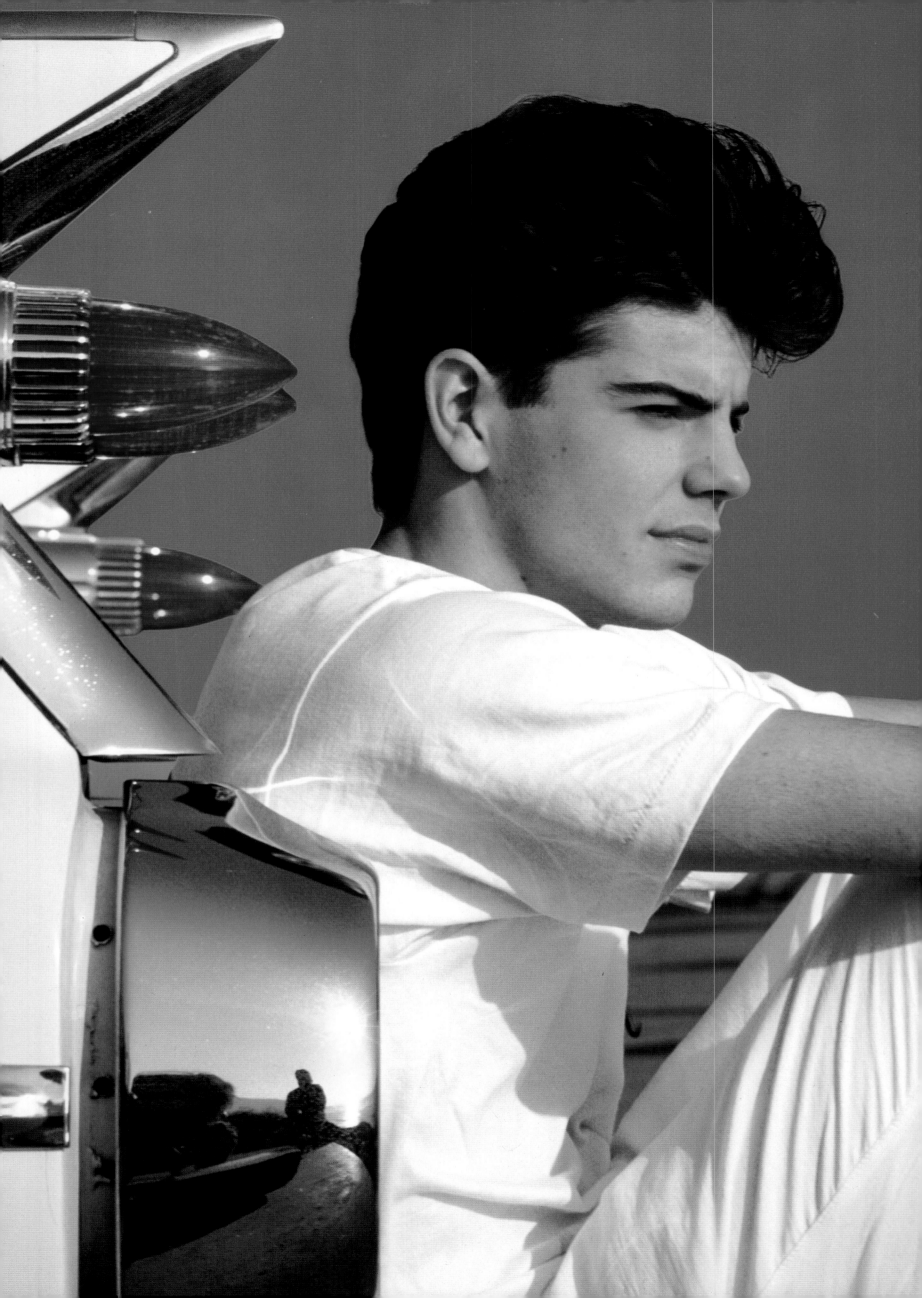

Elvis had moves I've never seen before, only he could do them because he's Elvis. I want to have moves that are completely Jordan.

I feel very secure around Dick; I always feel like he's looking out for me. His faith in me gives me a lot of confidence.

If I'm recording
a song and it's not
coming out perfect,
it's not going
on the record!

Sometimes it's hard to

make sense of all this.

d

donnie

Making love is so special...almost like the best feeling in the world. You have all the happiness there is right in your arms. I love to be in love.

I love

kissing. I'm not afraid to kiss
anyone. I'm not afraid of
homosexuality...I'm not one
but I'm just not afraid of it.
I know who and what I
am so it doesn't matter
if I go up to a guy
friend and hug him.

I am living my life the best way I

know how.

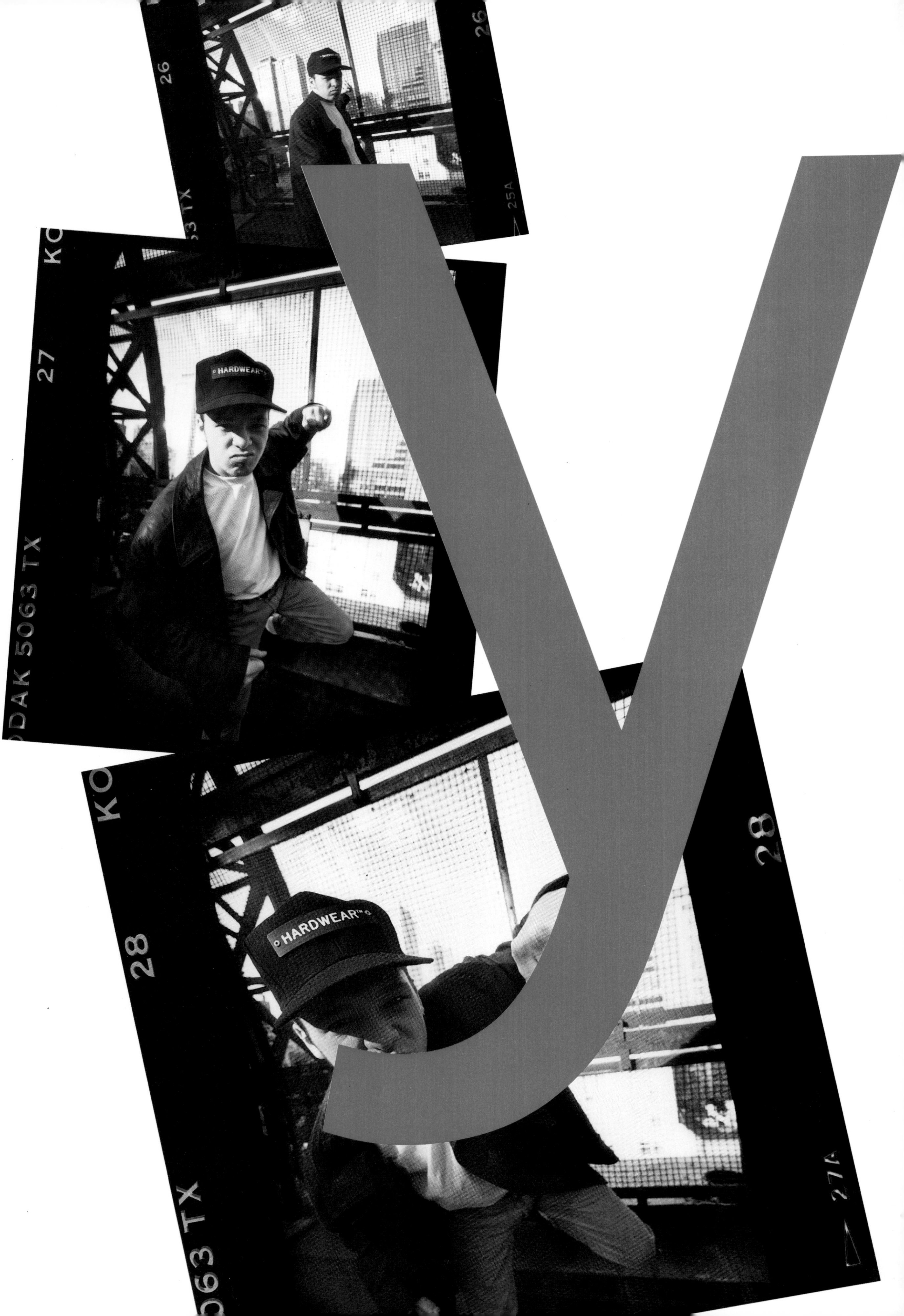
y
HARDWEAR
HARDWEAR
ODAK 5063 TX
063 TX
26
25A
27
28
27A

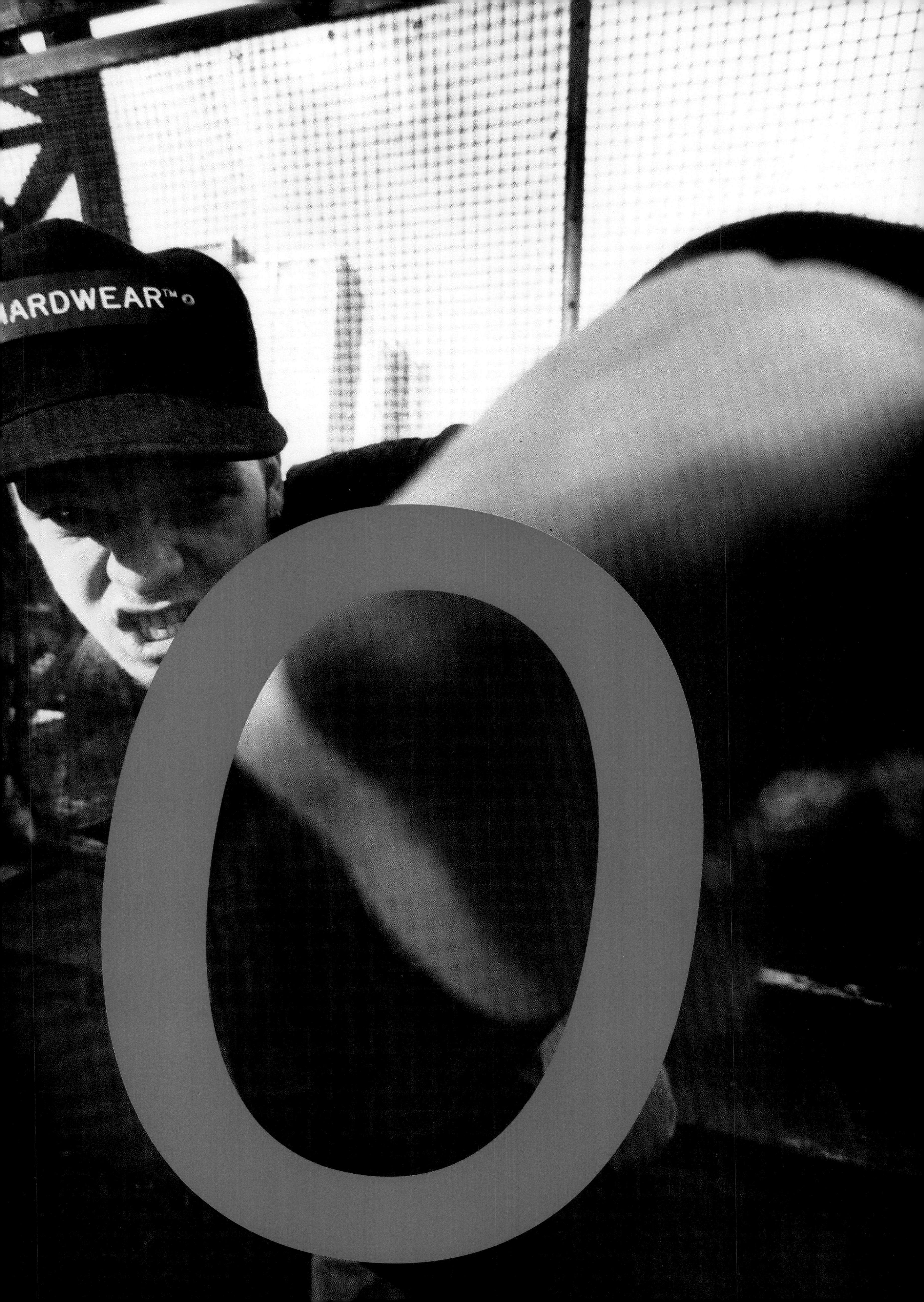
ARDWEAR™
O

I'm a person who wants to be understood. Maybe that's why I'm so outspoken.

I don't want people to see me as pop star of New Kids On The Block-goody-two-shoes-wholesome boy. I don't want them to see me as angry youth. I just want them to see me as Donnie Wahlberg.

If it were up to me, I wouldn't really practice for a tour. I'd just get up there and do it.

The fans accept me for

what I am.

I've worked
hard for my success.
I've paid my dues.

The whole peace sign business is like a hype...peace is what I believe in...not just the sign itself...but the peace sign I wear doesn't mean that I won't defend myself. I'll always fight for what I believe in.

Racism exists now because of the society we're living in. America hasn't come close to living up to its reputation. The reason there is white music and black music today is because black artists were never given a fair shake in the mainstream market.

I would love to see everyone happy and me right up there

being happy with them.

jonathan

Is there anything you want that you don't have?

I don't need anything materialistic

...maybe a new nose.

God doesn't make perfect humans and if he did,

it'd be a boring world.

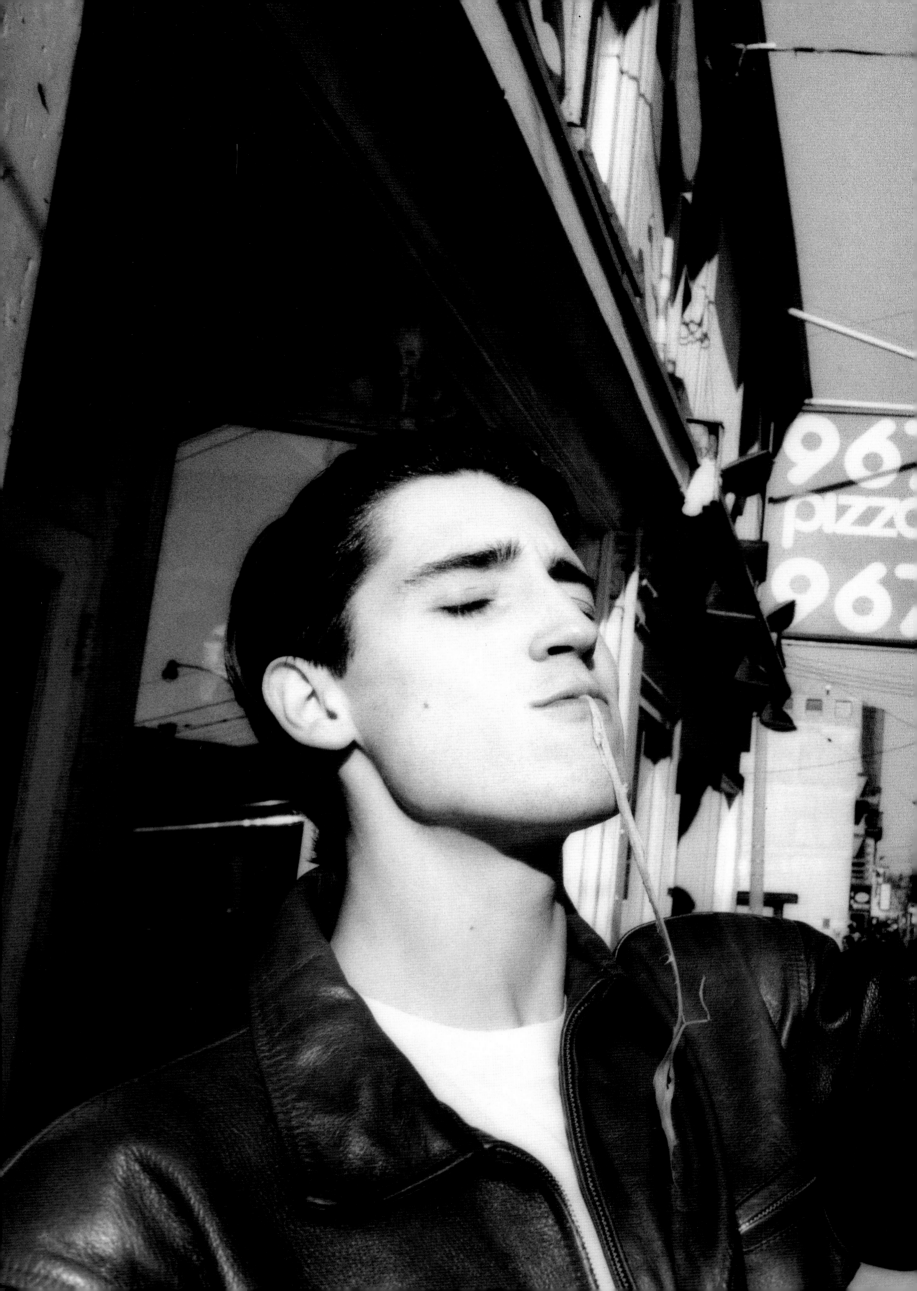

One time I was in a pizza restaurant...
the waitress stopped and just looked at me
and I got mad...that's probably the
worst thing...the privacy thing...
people don't see you as human anymore...
they don't think you do human things.

I'm happiest when I'm outdoors. I like to be a part of nature. Our environment is suffer-ing and that frightens me. I worry that if we don't take care now, it will be too late.

I like to just go off by myself.

Who did I idolize
when I was a kid?
Rob Lowe –
because every
one thought he
was so cute.
I always want-
ed to be the
handsome dude
and be on the
covers of
magazines.

A lot of times I get into an argument with my mother about taking aspirin or cough medicine. I tell her I don't need it because God made our bodies to take care of themselves. I tell her they didn't have medicine in the old days and she says that's why people died in their twenties.

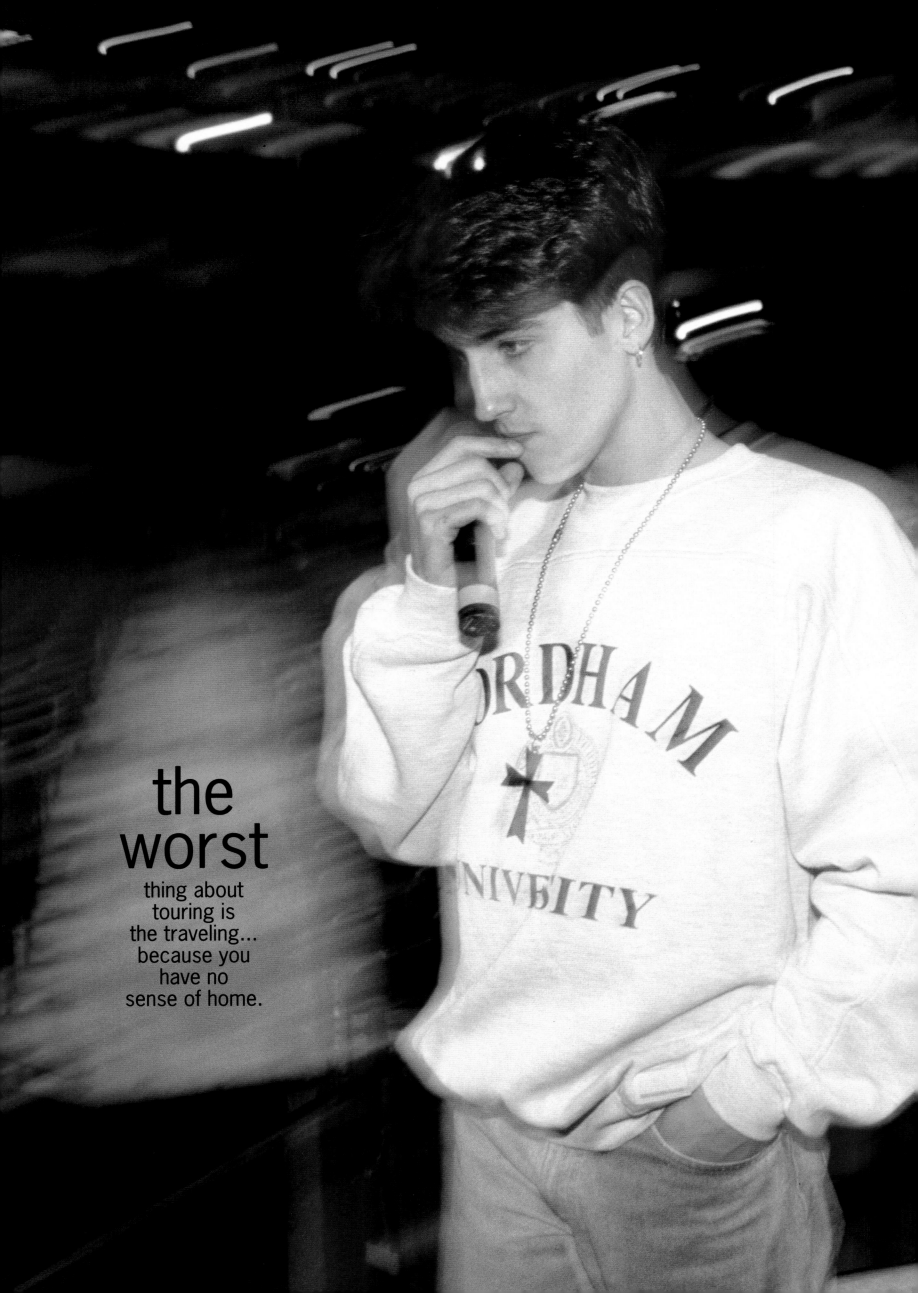

the
worst
thing about
touring is
the traveling...
because you
have no
sense of home.

I think romance is very sweet. I don't think there's too much of it out there these days. Men try to be too macho.

I've lost a lot of friends over my brother. People would always ask me do I love him. And I'd say "Do you love your brother?"

I always dreamed of being very famous...

I think
God is what-
ever you
conjure up
in your mind.
Maybe God
is your
conscience.

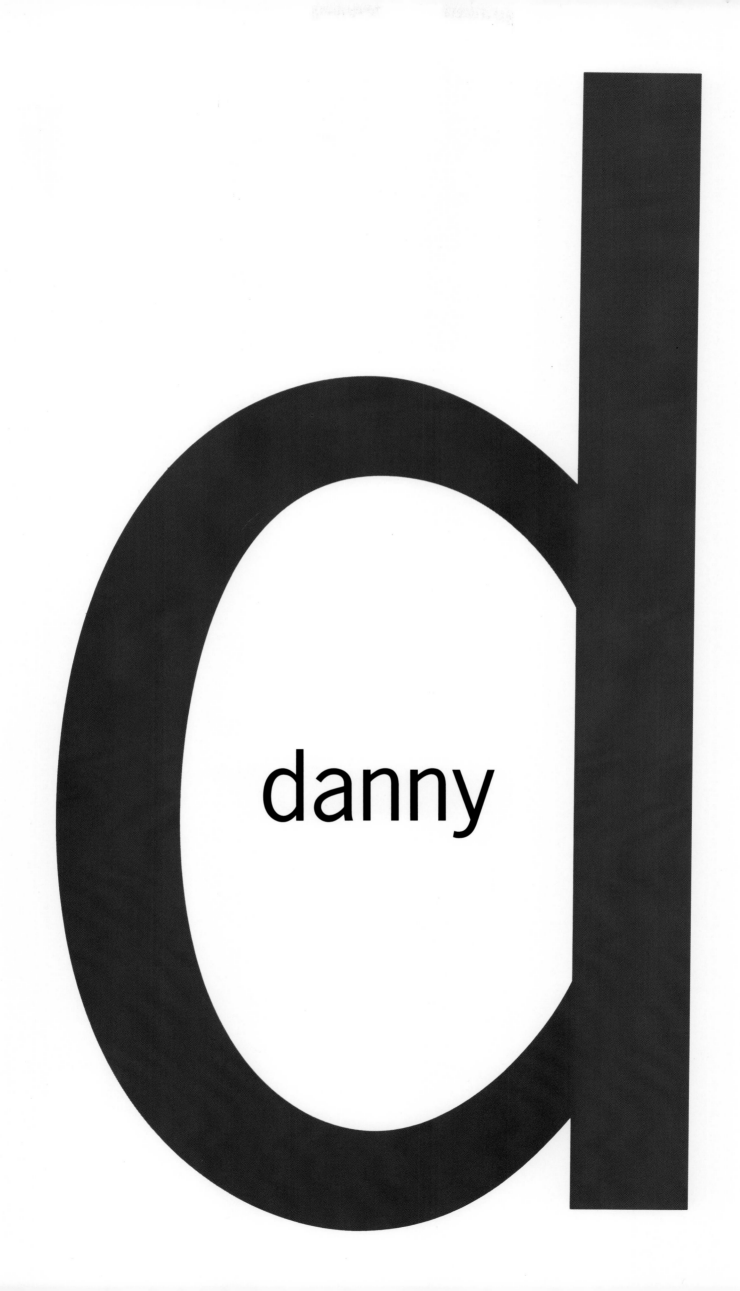
danny

All the violence
in the streets now
with the gangs...
that all comes back
to kids not having
enough places to
go or things to do.

I had a job

up until two years ago this May. I delivered airline tickets. I had left school because I wanted to concentrate more on the group but my father made me get a job. Our record was out and I was hearing it on the radio while delivering the tickets.

There's so much going on in our lives right now. We just gotta worry about our careers and keep what we're doing going. Later on we can all fall in love and settle down.

There's a big difference

between sex and making love. I'm not gonna say that I've never had sex because I'm 21 years old. When you have sex with someone, there is this feeling after like why did I do that, because sex is something that should be taken seriously. You shouldn't have sex with someone you don't care about. When you make love with someone, you want to be with that person because they are special to you. That's the difference.

I wouldn't say I come out and just tell a total all-out lie. I never try to deceive a person, but it might be something that slips out...like when I'm talkin' with the guys and I tell them I was checkin' out this girl and she was checkin' me out ...when she probably just looked at me and I exaggerated a little.

The worst thing about being on the road is not being

Underground Posse · Puff · Puffzilla The Goat Brothers

around your family and friends...and packing and unpacking.

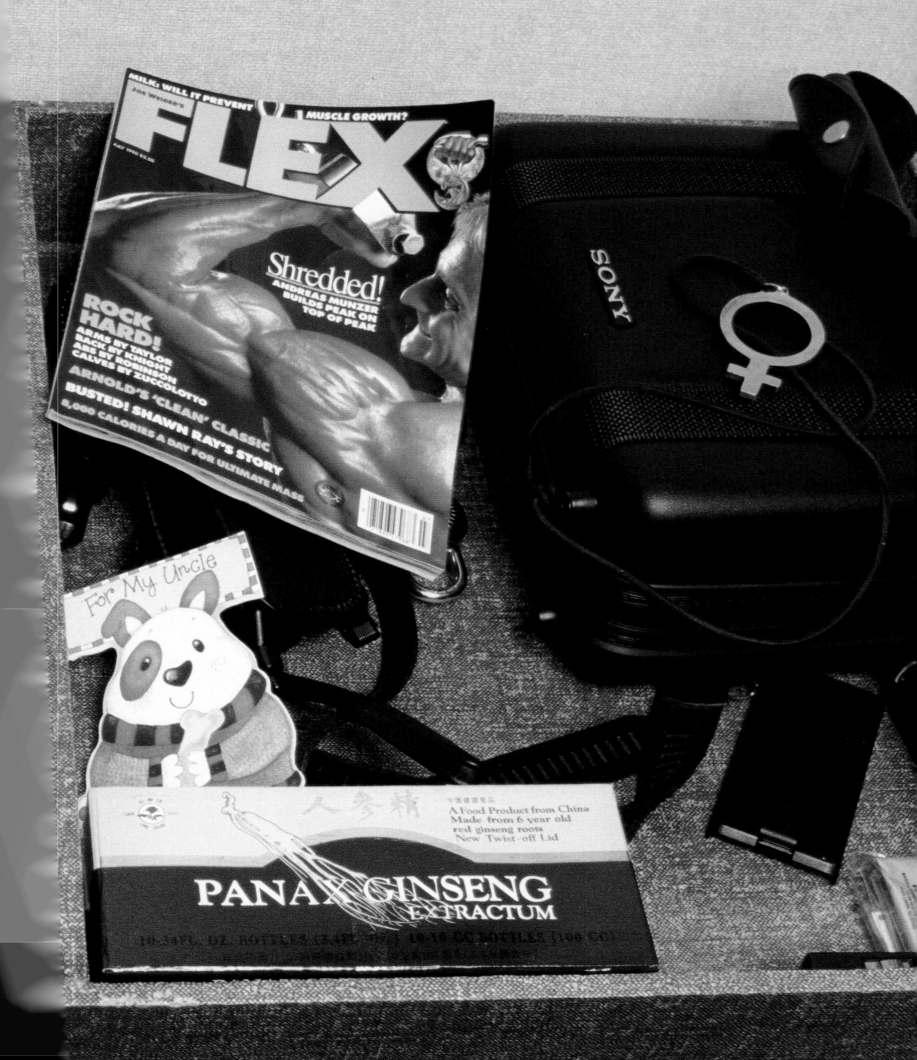

That bond between the son and his mother...it's so hard to explain. I love my mother so much.

How did you get started in bodybuilding?

I remember when we were doing the Right
Stuff video and one day I got up out of bed
and looked in the mirror and I kinda had a little
belly...I've always been in shape and I can't
have any of this...so I started working out.

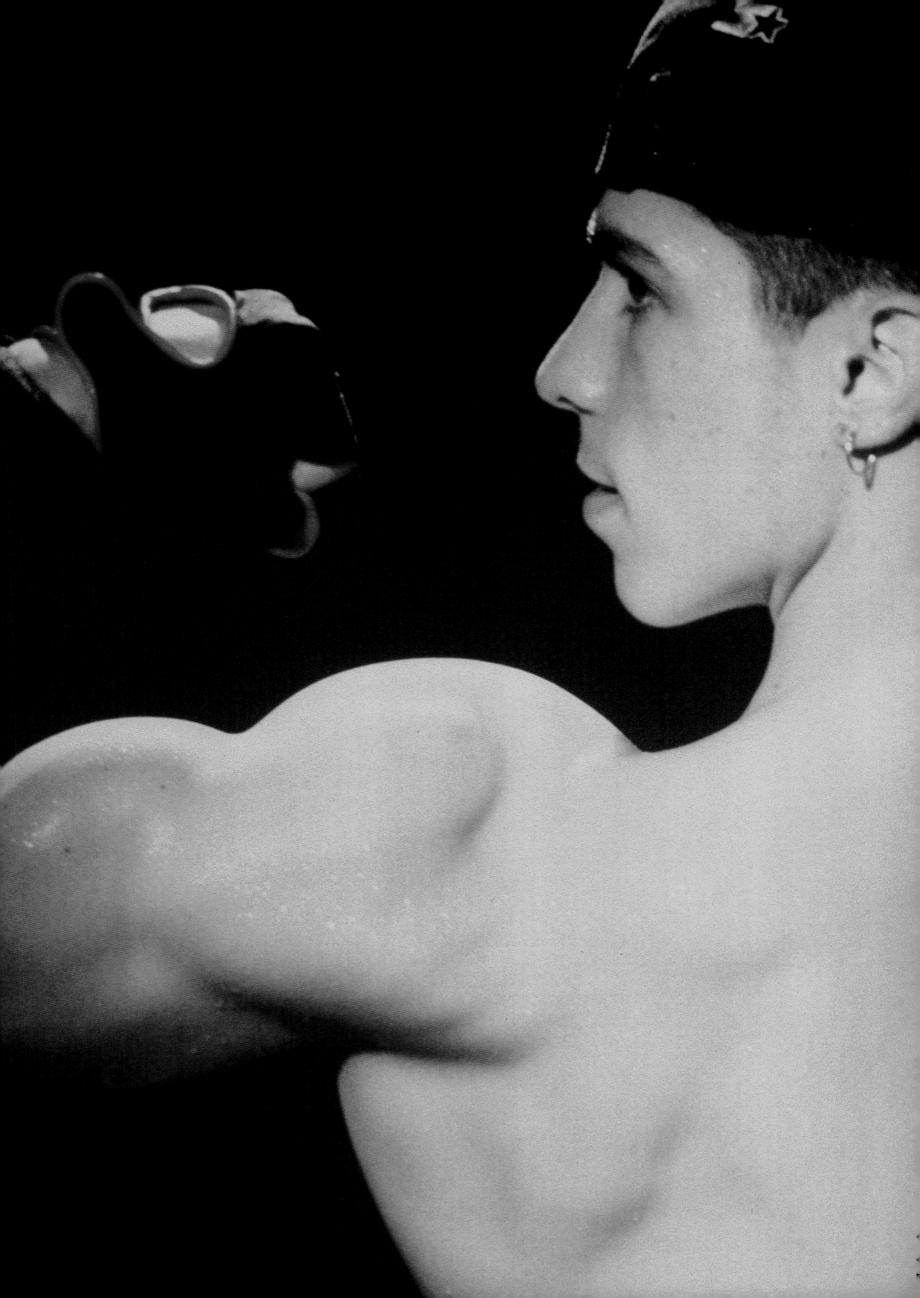

Do you think it does something for your mind?

Definitely, because when I wake up in the morning and go work out, I just put my mind on the gym and nothing else. Once it's over I feel great, I feel like my day's just started.

We're all wise beyond

our years.

joseph

Paris was the best thing that ever happened to me on the road. Once you get into Paris, your mood changes and you get enthralled by it. You get all romantic and you just want to sing Italian love songs even though you're in France.

When you're having a good show, it's the best feeling. You feel like you have the world in the palm of your hand.

Madonna...and ever since I saw her show...I admire her because she does what she wants to do...and she's the boss and she runs the show and she's really talented...and I admire her...and I think that when you admire someone, you see yourself doing what they are doing...
I just dreamt of Madonna...but it was the craziest dream because my parents were at a bar and they never drink and I was with Madonna and she was kissing me and I was thinking this was real dope and all of a sudden she turned into my sister Jean...it was crazy...and then I woke up...you can quote me on this...I'm gonna get hooked up with Madonna and she's gonna fall head over heels for me...Watch!

Who would you be and why?

I try to guide them, teach them, reduce their insecurities. No matter how much money or fame they have, I want them to be good people. – Dick Scott

It's funny because my father molded me for this business. We used to ride around and listen to Frank Sinatra, Al Jolson and Nat King Cole and just sing songs all the way home. I always liked Frank Sinatra because of his smooth and cool attitude. He isn't the greatest singer on earth and I'm not either but I think that I'm a good entertainer–that's what Frank is and I see that in myself…so that's why I guess I admire Frank Sinatra.

Fred Astaire on

was a great da

wasn't old blue

the other hand

ncer... but he

eyes.

Regardless of how much people work at it, and how much talent there is, it's still destiny.

My father
would laugh
at all
this gold.

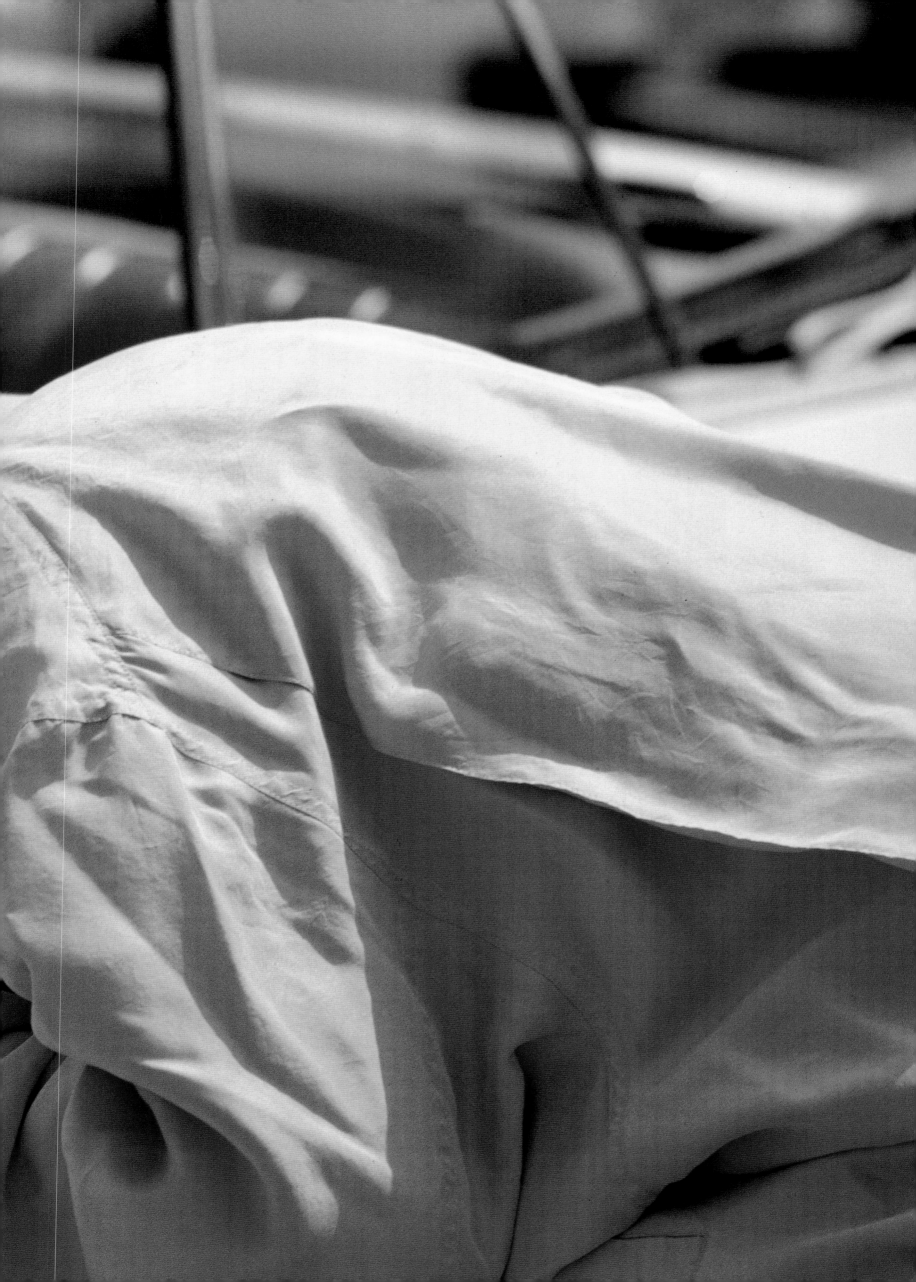

I was shy and just a

youngster...I like growing up.

She used to be my conscience. Whenever I wanted to do something, I'd think twice and ask myself what my mother would say. She wanted me to be a priest, but it doesn't really matter to her so long as I'm a good person.

fans

You are
beautifu

you

than I lo

so

l. I love

more

ve life.

You
looked
so good
today.
I hope I
didn't
annoy you
by follow-
ing you.
I wish I
could just
be your
friend.

When a black kid and a white kid grow up together, they don't care what color they are. – Joe

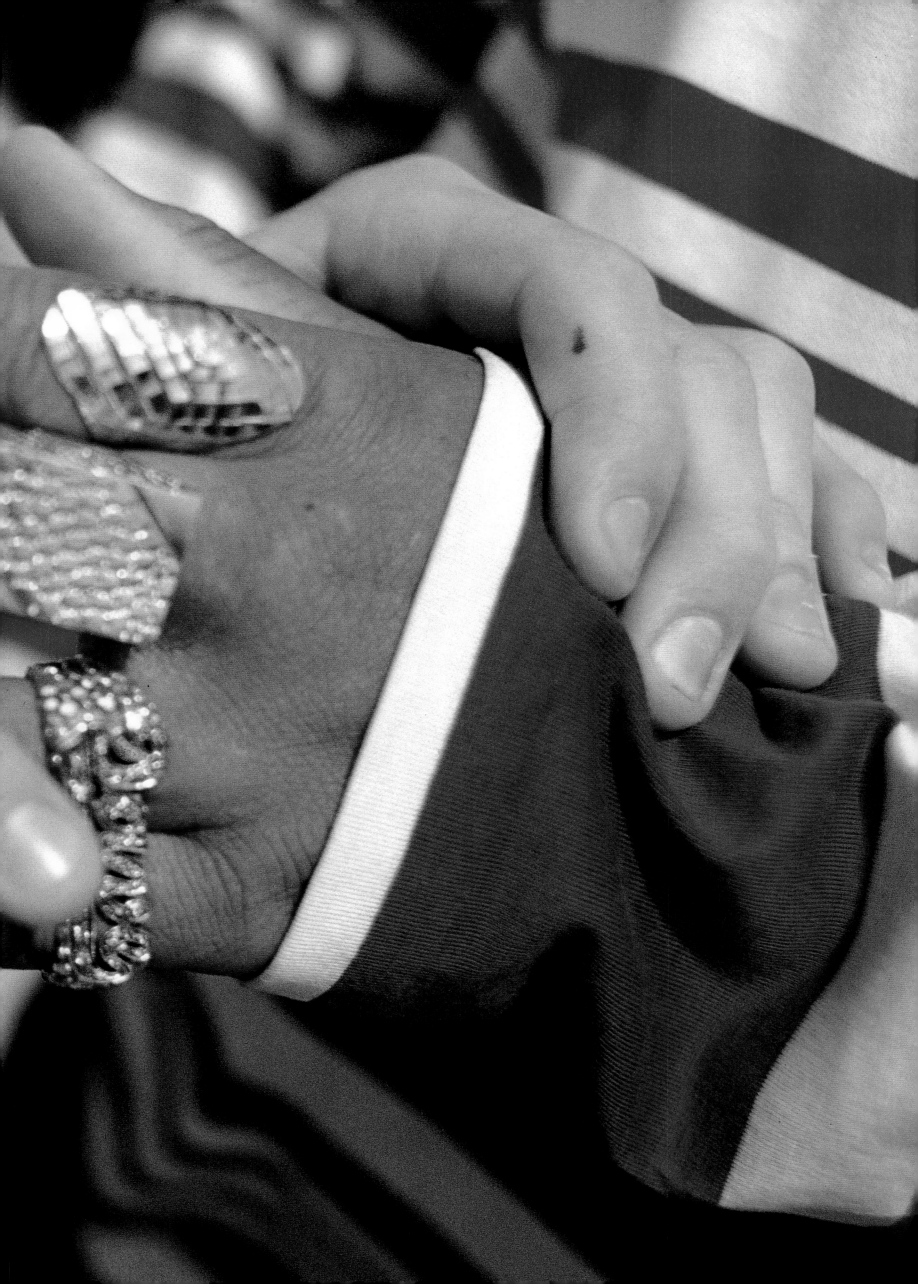

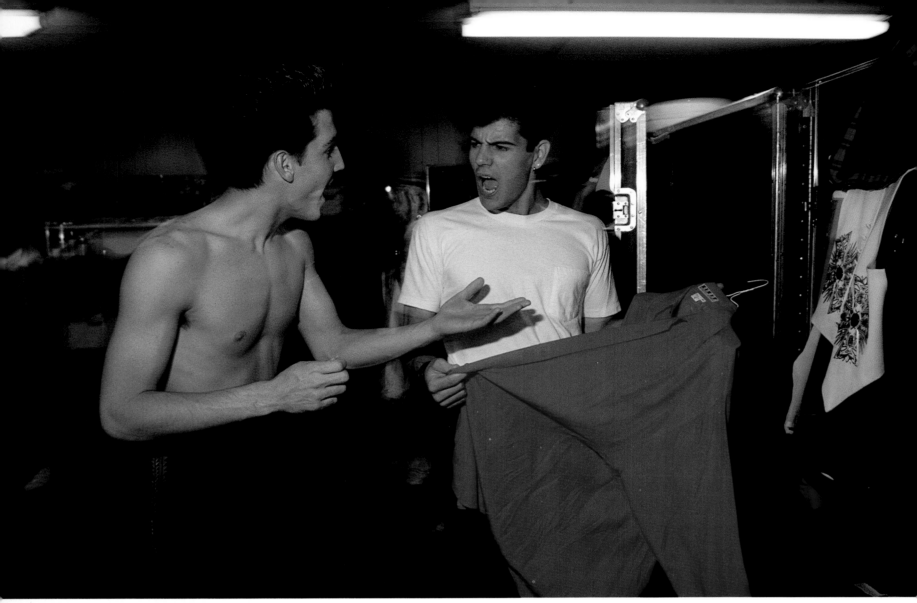

It works because they're

themselves. – Peter Work

90% of
the time
when I
think of
Jon,
I smile.

Everything that involves the New Kids is important to me. The music side, the stage side, the business side. I want to be responsible for all of it. When we're talking about something serious, I can be over in the corner, doodling with my hair. People might think I'm not listening, but I am, and at the end of the meeting I'll say something that makes total sense. I like to spring things on people. Surprise 'em. – Jordan

I hated my nickname.
I tried to change it to some
real hard street name,
but it never stuck. The Kids
didn't even know that my
nickname was Biscuit, until
one night someone told them
and they were all over the
floor. They thought it was the
funniest thing in the world.
The Kids have made it
a household name and now
Biscuit promotes
peace and love.

A lot of people think I'm real mean, but some people can read me behind these glasses and I wonder, how do they know?

— Biscuit

Donnie and I are a lot alike and really different at the same time. If we were both civil rights leaders I'd be Martin Luther King and he'd be Malcolm X. – Jordan

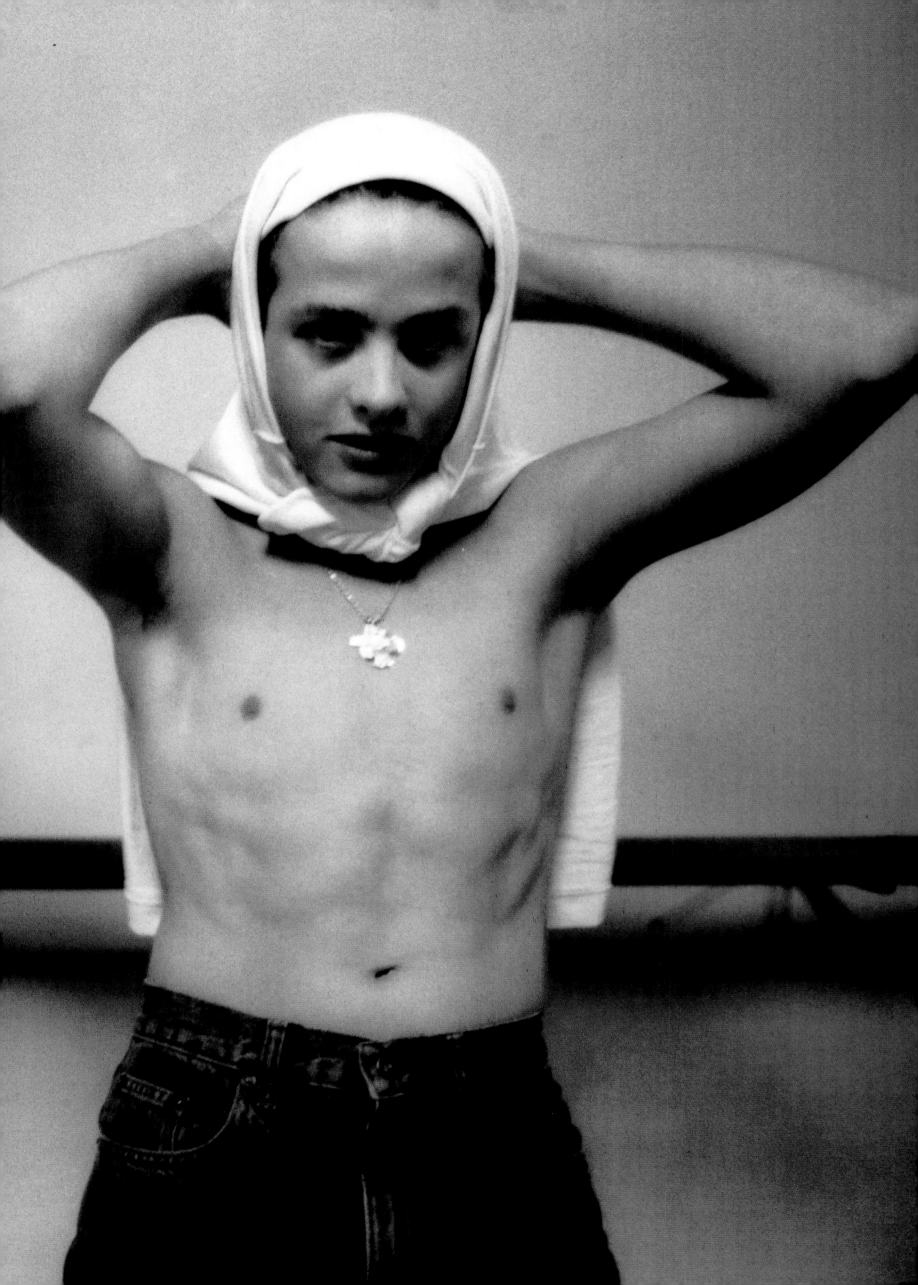

Jon on Jordan: He makes me proud...he always puts a smile on my face. I admire him more than myself. I got arrested once, for sticking up for my younger brother. It was when I was younger...this policeman was accusing Jordan of something he didn't do...so I walked

up to the policeman and said what's your problem and he said I ain't got a problem and he just said come with me and

he threw me in the police car and took me to the station.

Danny is bolted to the earth. If I ever feel pressured, he brings me back to reality. Danny just lays it down.
– Jordan

A lot of people see Donnie as a macho person, but I think he's one of the most sensitive people ever. – Jon

Joe's real mature. He experiences the same things we do. He's seventeen going on twenty one. – Danny

Jordan inspires me, pumps me up. We have a lot of things in common. When I'm feeling down and blue, I can always go to Jordan. – Joe

Jon and I can get each other mad, but we always make up, and we never hold a grudge. – Donnie

dream, so you leave and half for real life.
– Jordan

The New Kids Staff

Peter Work
Johnny Wright
Julie Hooker
Robo
Biscuit
Cathy McLaughlin
Alan Grissinger
Brad Bowman
Uncle Rob
Dana Allyson
Mark O'Dowd
Kim Glover
Win Wilford
Sam Owens
Joe Pappalardo
Andrea Ciucci
Nina Valery
Rodney Fisher
Dennis Armstead
Nick Gold
Marianne Visconti
Mary Alford
Hoss and the Gang

Photography Assistance

Nikon Professional Services
Gail Dailey
Elaine Brandin
Clone-A-Chrome
Richard Paganello
Todd Stone
John Beaudin
George Robertson
Todd Flashner

thank you

Special thanks
to Ray DeMoulin,
Dick Scott,
the Kids, the fans,
my parents,
and the power of
love without
which this book
would not exist.

All The New Kids' Families

Special Advice

Charles Styles
Barry Rosenthal
Ike Williams
Ben Zinkin
Gary Stiffelman
Roger Rubin
Ellen Nieves
Larry Busacca
Laura Giammarco
Elvis

Editing

Chris Dougherty
Choo-Choo Kim
Ilana Haiken

Design

Frank Gargiulo
Scott Frommer